Tl

The Worth of a Penny

by

John E. Silver

Cover designed by Jonte' Silver

1

Copyright © 2010 by JonHod Publishing

ISBN-13: 978-0-9817374-9-2

ISBN-10:   0-9817374-9-2

This book was printed in the United States of America.

Scripture reference was taken from the King James Version and the New Living Translation.

History of the penny, courtesy of www.wikipedia.org.

Acknowledgements

I would like to take this opportunity to first and foremost thank God for sending His only Son Jesus to die for a sinner like me. Truly this would not be possible without Him. I would like to thank God for my parents James and Jennie Silver, for without God using them there would be no me. I want to also thank God for my three siblings Janie, James and Jean Silver, who have always loved and cared for me unconditionally. I also would like to thank God for my nieces, nephews and all family alike. I truly want to say thank you to God for my friend, my companion, my pillar, my support; my voice when I am speechless, my courage when I am discouraged and for being the Eve that God created just for me. She really is the needle that fits in the grooves of my record and without her I would have no sound. I am speaking of no one other than my wife, Dena— *I love you always*. I also want to thank God for my three sons Kareem, Jonte' and Jahod, who have been very supportive of me. I thank God for my church family in so many ways. May God continue to bless you. But there is one person in particular, whom I would like to express my deepest thanks to for being very instrumental and encouraging in my finishing this book for the glory of God's beautiful name. Mrs. Corine Grooms. Thank you so much for everything, God has so many special blessings with your name on them, Amen.................................

3

This author is available for signings, seminars and speaking engagements. For more information, contact:

JonHod Publishing Services
Web site: www.jonhod.com
Email: info@jonhod.com
publishjpc@jonhod.com

Chapters

Introduction

Jesus in His unlimited acumen, invites you and me to take a very close look at a parable in the bible that talks about standing idle and doing nothing all day. I believe that so many Christians in this present day find themselves in this same posture of redundancy. We go to church idle. We go to our jobs idle. We even live a life that is idle. In other words, we exhaust all of our energy on self while remaining idle in one place—never using it for the purpose at demand. You see, in this parable, Jesus speaks about a householder going out early in the morning to hire workers to work in his vineyard. Once He hires them, He then makes an agreement with the "workers" to pay them one denarius, or should I say one penny, for a day's labor of work. What is so profound about this parable is that the householder agrees to pay them a denarius or one penny. Today it seems as if everyone wants to make the big dollars, but do less working. We want monetary advancement, without voluntary involvement. But I have come to tell you that "more money" will not make you happy. But working for the Master will cause you to rejoice in the God of your salvation. Do you remember the "registered letter" you received in your heart? Sure you do, you signed for it when you said yes to Jesus. So now open up the letter and receive your true blessings and "revelations" that can only come from a God who sits high, but continues to love low. Now back to the parable, better yet………. Jesus can tell the story much better than I can. He starts out in this comportment.

> *"For the kingdom of heaven is like unto a man that is an householder, which went out early in the morning to hire labourers into His vineyard. And when He had agreed with the labourers for a penny a day, He sent them into His vineyard. And he went out about the third hour, and saw others standing idle in the marketplace, And said unto them; Go ye also into the vineyard, and whatsoever is right I will give you. And they went their way. Again He went out about the sixth and ninth hour, and did likewise. And about the eleventh hour He went out, and found others standing idle, and saith unto them, Why stand ye here all the day idle? They say unto Him, Because no man hath hired us. He saith unto to them, Go ye also into the vineyard; and whatsoever is right, that shall ye receive. So when even was come, the Lord of the vineyard saith unto his steward, Call the labourers, and give them their hire, beginning from the last unto the first. And when they came that were hired about the eleventh hour, they received every man a penny (Matthew Chapter 20:1-9).*

Now the word *idle* comes from the root Greek word *Argos,* which means, *not busy, doing nothing, just shooting the breeze, dormant; latent, unmoving or quiescent.* I think you get the idea regarding this word *idle.* How about you, do you find yourself standing idle all day doing nothing in your spiritual life? Or does your personal life overshadow your spiritual life at this moment? But if you will give God His time and your mind, something will change in your life—but only if you are willing to…

> *Commit thy works unto the Lord, and thy thoughts shall be established (Proverbs 16:3). Amen.*

God's Wonderful Revelation

The worth of a penny………. I would like to ask you some very important questions, as it relates to the worth of a penny. If I handed you one penny and asked you how much it was worth, you would probably say one cent. Perhaps, if I asked you to go and exchange it for something more valuable, you would probably think I was out of my mind. Why? Because no matter how we perceive the penny it will always remain as one cent. So now I would like to awaken your perception sensors as it relates to the *worth of a penny*. I am just so excited about sharing this wonderful, but yet evolutional revelation from our God that I do not think that I will be able to contain myself without having to move to quickly to the meat or the best part first. Now in order to understand this wonderful revelation from our God, your mind needs to throw out the predictable way of thinking. Listen to the Apostle Paul as he penned this truth in the book of Romans.

> *And be not conformed to this world; but be ye transformed by the **renewing of your mind,** that ye may prove what is that good, and acceptable, and perfect, will of God (Romans 12:2).*

Having said that, let's continue with this wonderful revelation from our God. You see, writers are blessed with a gift to write. I am not gifted in that sense, but I am spirited; meaning, the Holy Spirit is leading and guiding me every step of the way. Because this is true, I will exclaim with great joy like the Psalmist when he declares that we should ***make a joyful noise unto the Lord, all ye lands!*** *(Psalms 100:1).*

I figured I may as well shout in the beginning of this wonderful revelation God has given me for He is worthy to be praised.

I am a mailman for the United States Postal Service, with over 20 years of professional service rendered to the public. I have great dignity and pride for my job, so my dedication to this assignment would not surprise those who know me. One day while walking on my route past so many pennies, I began to think about their treatment. They were tossed out, trampled on and left to survive on their own. That's when the light came on, that's when I had an epiphany—a God given revelation. I became so excited that I just could not wait to get home and share the good news with my family. From that day forward, God has been revealing this wonderful truth to me about lost and seemingly worthless pennies.

But this is only possible when we ***study to shew thyself approved unto God, a workman that needeth not to be ashamed, rightly dividing the word of truth*** *(2 Timothy 2:15).*

After I studied His word, it became my responsibility for carrying out the commands and teachings of Christ. Sounds very simple—and it is! You and I have a written record of this command, and teaching from Christ. In *Matthew 28: 18-20* we read:

> *And Jesus came and spake unto them, saying, "All power is given unto Me in heaven and in earth. Go ye therefore, and teach all nations, baptizing them in the name of the Father, and of the Son, and of the Holy Ghost: Teaching them to observe all things whatsoever I have commanded you; and, lo, I am with you alway, even unto the end of the world. Amen.*

Now I can hear you thinking, how does this scripture tie in with worthless pennies? And I can tell you it has more depth than what you might understand at this moment. But I pray that by the time we reach the end of the revelation, we will all be the better for His name's glory and honor. So before I continue with this wonderful revelation from our God, let's take a look back over the history of the worthless penny that we take for granted—with no true regard for its importance or value in the world today. We will take a look at **Wikipedia,** as for it will help to bring some clarity about this "worthless" penny.

From Gold to Bronze

When Britain was under Roman rule, most of Britain used the coin-based monetary system that was used by the Roman Empire, but their system of coinage soon changed after the Romans left. As the invading Anglo-Saxons began to settle and establish their own kingdoms, some started to make gold coins based on the old Roman designs or designs copied from the coins used in the Frankish kingdoms. Their monetary system had several serious flaws. First, gold was so valuable that even the smallest coins were very valuable, being used only in large transactions. Second, gold was very rare, and this rarity prevented such coins from being common enough to use for even large transactions.

Between the years 640 and 670 AD, there seems to have been a movement by the Anglo-Saxons to use less pure gold in coins. This made the coins appear paler, decreased their value, and may have increased the number that could be made, but it still didn't solve the problems of value and scarcity of coins made mostly of gold.

The first pennies

Up to this time, no Anglo-Saxon coin had been minted in any metal besides gold. However, around the year 680, a new type of small silver coin appeared which some have identified them as "sceattas" or "sceat", but this was probably an error. Sceatta was a specific measurement of a precious metal. These new coins were actually called pennies. In 1257, Henry III minted a gold penny which had the value of twenty silver pence. The weight and value of the silver penny steadily declined from 1300 onwards. The penny, with a few exceptions, was the only coin issued in England until the introduction of the gold florin by Edward III in 1343. In 1527 the Tower pound of 5,400 grains was abolished and replaced by the pound of 5760 grains.

Halfpence and farthings became a regular part of the coinage at that time, money which was created by cutting pennies to halves and quarters for trade purposes, a practice said to have originated in the reign of Ethelred II. The last coinage of silver pence for general circulation was in the reign of Charles II. Since then silver pence have only been coined for issue as royal alms on Maundy Thursdays.

First use of copper

Copper halfpence were first issued in Charles II's reign, but it was not until 1797, in the reign of George III, that copper pence were minted. George III's copper penny weighed 1 oz. Copper twopences were issued weighing 2 oz in the same year, but they were found too cumbersome and so were discontinued.

The penny that was brought to the Cape was a large coin 41 mm in diameter, 5 mm thick and 2 oz. On it was Britannia with a trident in her hand. The English called this coin The Cartwheel Penny due to its large size and raised rim, but the Capetonians referred to it as the Devil's Penny as they assumed that only the Devil used a trident. The coins were very unpopular due to their large weight and size.

The first copper coins that Boulton minted for the British Government are known as 'cartwheels', because of their large size and raised rims. The Soho Mint struck 500 short tons (450 t) of these penny and two penny pieces in 1797, and issued further copper coins for the Government in 1799, 1806 and 1807. All together the Mint produced over £600,000 worth of copper official English coinage as well as separate copper coins for Ireland and the Isle of Man.

On June 6, 1825 Sir Charles Somerset issued a proclamation that only British Sterling would be legal tender in the Cape. The new British coins (which were introduced in England in 1816), among them being the shilling, six pence of silver, the penny, half penny and quarter penny in copper, were introduced to the Cape. Later two shilling, four penny and three penny coins were added to the coinage. The size and denomination of the 1816 British coins, with the exception of the four-penny coins, were used in South Africa until 1960.

Use of bronze

In 1860 bronze pennies were introduced in place of copper ones, though they were not entirely made of bronze; instead were made of an alloy containing 95 parts of copper, 4 of tin, and 1 of zinc. The weight was also reduced: 1 lb of bronze was coined into 48 pennies, versus 1 lb of copper which was coined into 24 pennies (www.wikipedia.org).

State of Urgency
(Loo-Lea-Lif)

So now as you can see, the penny is among the lowest denomination of coins in circulation today in the United States. Wow! I expect you did not realize that the penny had such a rich history behind it. They say that knowledge is power, so then wisdom and understanding become the two levers that help to turn on true revelation. I pray that this will open up our minds so that we may absorb all of God's wonderful blessings. Please allow me to share this with you. What you and I understand will determine how we see God's beautiful revelations unfolding right before our very eyes. Knowledge, wisdom and understanding should be a life-long search for the believer that is in Christ Jesus. We should seek after her with all of our heart, mind, body and soul. Here is how the *proverbial* writer proclaims it, in the *fourth division verses 1-10:*

> *Hear, ye children, the instruction of a father, and attend to know understanding. For I give you good doctrine, forsake ye not my law. For I was my father's son, tender and only beloved in the sight of my mother. He taught me also, and said unto me, let thine heart retain my words; keep my commandments, and live. Get wisdom, get understanding: forget it not; neither decline from the words of my mouth. Forsake her not, and she*

shall preserve thee: love her, and she shall keep thee. Wisdom is the principal thing; therefore get wisdom: and with all thy getting get understanding. Exalt her, and she shall promote thee: she shall bring thee to honour, when thou dost embrace her. She shall give to thine head an ornament of grace: a crown of glory shall she deliver to thee. Hear, O my son, and receive my sayings; and the years of thy life shall be many.

Now let us turn our attention back to the subject matter at hand—the penny. I would first like to point out the *state of urgency* I found some of these worthless pennies. Some were found in the dirt, others in puddles of water, bushes, on the streets, in dark alleys, and on the sidewalks. I even found some glued together by the harsh conditions of time. To put it quite simply, there were lost pennies everywhere. But I only noticed the pennies when I began to **loolealif.** Yes I did, I made up my own word and it sounds like something, amen (laugh). But this is really what this word means, **looking, leaning, and lifting.** Now all of these verbs take action by looking, make action by leaning, so as to get a reaction from lifting. But out of the three, I found that the **leaning** and **lifting** became my most difficult challenge in this entire process of finding these lost and worthless pennies. I will speak a little bit more about that later on.

Looking

Now it is quite amazing to me when one is able to *look* down and see so much more than what is really visible to the naked eye. Here is the first pivotal point of this wonderful revelation from our God. You must first *look* down to see them. Let me repeat the first part of that phrase again. You must first look down to see them. You see I have yet to find a single penny while *looking* up. I know that we have been taught that we should keep our heads up when we are walking, and that is true, but in this case I am asking you to do just the opposite. By learning to *look* down it helps the believer to be mindful of where God has delivered him or her from. No I am not suggesting that we look paltry and broken down as if we are not children of the most-high God. What I am suggesting is that we should never forget where our God has delivered us from. Now just for the sake of remembrance, let's read from the word of our God together.

> *But ye are a chosen generation, a royal priesthood, an holy nation, a peculiar people; that ye should shew forth the praises of Him who hath called you out of darkness into His marvelous light (1 Peter 2:9).*

God is so awesome in the way that he communicates with His Children. The word declares that He has called you and me out of darkness into His marvelous light. You know before cell phones and all of this advanced technology, we communicated by calling out to each other. Also, growing up in the city has taught me many other valuable lessons in life. Every time I would go outside to play, my mother or father would say to me, *"When the street lights turn on, I am only going to call your name one time."* Once I heard my name, I would make my way home in a hurry. But take notice of something in this example with me. I mentioned that when the street lights came on my mother or father would call out my name, so that I might make my way home. But our God responds in a different way. He calls out for you and me when the lights are out, *not on*.

Have you ever been lost in the dark, and had no idea of which way to go or turn? It is a lonely feeling and a frightening reality for one to face in life. Normally when one is lost in the natural sense of darkness, the very first thing we will do is feel our way through the darkness; only to discover that we cannot find our way out without some kind of guidance or assistance. God calls out for you and me in the mist of darkness and He shines His eternal wattage of love into our hearts. We then run to Him for protection and shelter and He receives the lost soul with opened arms. The bible reports it this way, *"**I am the way**" (John 14:6a)* declares Jesus. And because He is the way, we can rest and be assured that He will bring us safely out of darkness and into His marvelous light. I would like to share with you a short story in relation to one being lost and found by such a loving family. There is a young lady on my route who loves dogs very much. One day, as I was making my rounds in front of her house, three poodles came out of nowhere. Quite naturally I was startled and caught off guard, but she assured me that they were harmless. She then shared with me that one of the dogs was from an adoption agency, and how glad she was that he was now a part of her family. But as she was sharing her story with me, I took notice of the dog that was adopted. I could see that both of his eyes were glowing, as if it was a foggy gray and white color. This really gathered my attention, but I could not help becoming inquisitive, so I asked the young lady what had happened to the dog that would cause his eyes to look that way. She answered without dithering. Her voice pitch changed from low to high, and I understood that this dog was important to her and that she was truly a dog lover. She went on to explain that when he was a puppy the prior owners kept him in a dark room all the time and never allowed him to go outside into the light. So therefore his pupils never developed and this caused him to go blind. So again I asked the young lady how then is he able to get around so well? She then replied that he learned how to follow the scent and the barks of the other dogs *(Jesus declares that- **I am the way**).* I was amazed at such a powerful, and yet moving story. How at one point of this dog's life he was blinded by being in total darkness, but now he has been saved by someone who truly loves him and cares for him, and now calls him by his new name. Now I want to share with you a brief grammar lesson in Greek. The word translated "out" is **"ek"**, and the word translated "called", is the word **"kalesantos**." The Greeks would put them together to form another word, *"ekklesia"* which means, "Called out" and refers to an assembly or gathering of people that has been called together. We too have been called out for a reason and for a purpose. When we come to understand this truth, we then respond to the Father's calling that He has on our lives by being obedient to His life changing word. There is ever more good news, as we continue to read in *1 Peter 2:10*. It seals for you and me the truth of our joy and salvation in Jesus. It speaks in this comportment.

> *Which in time past were not a people, but are now the people of God: which had not obtained mercy, but now have obtained mercy.*

You and I have gained so much from our wonderful Savior, who died on Calvary's cross. The cross of Calvary has amalgamated you and me back to the Father's perfect love. As if that was not enough, our Father continues to share His loving heart with you and me. It is because of Christ that we have been given mercy upon mercy and more mercy. And if we can always remember this truth, we will be very effective in our living for the Master who is our Savior, amen.

There was one part of the adopted dog story I did not share for a reason, so as to save it for this portion of the revelation. If you can remember a few lines back, I asked you to take a walk with me through the scriptures as we remember how good our God has been to us. He did this by bringing you and me out of darkness into His marvelous light. I was attempting to turn your praise level on high, so as to make certain that God would get all the glory. But I pray that you have come to understand this wonderful truth on your own. In the Gospel of *John 12:46,* Jesus speaks in this comportment.

> *I am come a light into the world, that whosoever believeth on Me should not abide in darkness.*

In spite of everything that adopted dog went through in his early stages of life, and having to have lived in so much darkness; he never gave up. He must have understood that there was more life to be lived, so he hung in there until he was rescued out of darkness. This dog now has so much joy and vivacity that it really caused me to step back and evaluate my own personal walk with the risen Savior. So now, as I look down on the ground, I am able to see so much more in relation to these so-called lost and worthless pennies. I have learned to walk in the light of Christ. The *Psalmist* declares it this way, in the *119th division, verse 105.*

> *Thy word is a lamp unto my feet, and a light unto my path.*

So with that being said you and I must always remember, *for we walk by faith, not by sight (2 Corinthians 5-7a).* So now I implore you to look down, as you live your life through Him. And He promises to guide your "mind, body and spirit" as we walk with Him by faith amen................

Leaning

Leaning down is another important step, in understanding this wonderful revelation from our God. It challenges you and me to make a choice; either to pick up the lost and worthless penny, or leave it—the choice is yours. This is the middle part of the decision making process. Whatever you choose to do will be very important for the next step, concerning these lost and worthless pennies. You will have three choices to make in a split second. So you must be ready to react at a moment's notice. Now for me, the choices became easier and easier. I would just look, lean, and lift—choice made. Only because I now understand that these lost and worthless pennies have so much value to me, and they should have value to you also. Now in order to move from one step to the next, by *looking, leaning, and lifting,* we need to understand how this process can work. It can, but only if we are willing to yield physically after we *look.* Sometimes when I am delivering the mail, the customer may have a certified letter that requires a signature. So while I am waiting for the customer to answer the door, I would find myself *leaning* on the porch railings so that I might relieve the tension from my legs, and back as I wait. *Leaning* seems to take away all of the tightness and tension. In other words I gain extra support when I would *lean* on the railings of the porch. Please follow me, because the Holy Spirit is *leaning* me at this very moment. I just believe that when I would *lean* down to pick up these lost and worthless pennies, I was giving it the support that it needed, so that it may have a fresh start and a new look on life. Allow me to make it plain—that it might be saved. Now imagine if I would have thought about my physical state at that moment. I would have missed the opportunity to give the penny the support it needed. But I made up my mind to change the way I was thinking, feeling, seeing and understanding these three important steps. Now *leaning* was probably the most crucial step, in the sense that I needed to move out of my own understanding and trust that God was really the one *leaning* not me. Sometimes in life, you will need to *lean* on someone in the natural. But in the spiritual, Jesus becomes our full support. Now let us read the word of our God together as He speaks of this wonderful truth for you and me.

> *Trust in the Lord with all thine heart; and lean not unto thy own understanding (Proverbs 3:5).*

So understanding is very critical for you and me, only if we are willing to trust our God at His Word. I remember some time back, when I was a young boy, I did an experiment with two small sticks. I wanted to see if any of the sticks would be able to stand on their own without the other stick having to provide some type of support. What I discovered was that neither one could stand on its own without having to *lean* on the other. Also neither of the sticks would be able to *lean* on each other without a level surface or base. What they really needed was a solid foundation. When you and I understand this truth, it will cause us to learn to *lean* on God and not our own understanding. We are then able to trust the solid foundation that is around us. Allow me to put it in this manner, according to the old Hymnologist. *On Christ the solid rock I stand all other ground is sinking sand.* Now I could have easily put the two sticks in the ground where the dirt was, but then there would be the test of life—storms, floods and heavy winds. Then what? Please continue to **lean** with me as I continue to **lean** with the help of the Holy Spirit.

> *Therefore whosoever heareth these sayings of mine, and doeth them, I will liken him unto a wise man, which built his house upon a rock: And the rain descended, and the floods came, and the winds blew, and beat upon that house; and it fell not: for it was founded upon a rock. And every one that heareth these sayings of mine, and doeth them not, shall be likened unto a foolish man, which built his house upon the sand: And the rain descended, and the floods came, and the winds blew, and beat upon that house; and it fell: and great was the fall of it.*

Now why was that scripture provided? I am so glad that you asked that question in your **leaning**. In the book of *Proverbs* you will discover a collection of pithy sayings that are saturated with three main words: *wisdom, knowledge, and understanding.* When we read the account according to *Matthew 7:24 thru 27,* Jesus shares with you and me a truth about understanding God's wonderful gift of wisdom as it relates to our solid foundation that is in Him. Now all of us have compared our lives to someone or something, only because we wanted to be like that person in some way. But look at how the Master describes you and me according to His word. In *Matthew 7:24a,* He declares:

> *Therefore whosoever heareth these sayings of mine, and doeth them, I will liken him unto a wise man.*

There is the connection from the book of *Proverbs 3:5* and the account in *Matthew 7:24-27.* So once you and I understand God's gift of wisdom, we are then able to **lean** and trust in Him according to His word, will, and way. How do we receive this wonderful gift of wisdom that I am speaking about? I am so glad that you asked. Here is the answer according to God's powerful word.

> *That the God of our Lord Jesus Christ, the Father of glory, may give unto you the spirit of wisdom and revelation in the knowledge of Him: The eyes of your understanding being enlightened; that ye may know what is the hope of His calling, and what the riches of the glory of His inheritance in the saints, And what is the exceeding greatness of His power to us-ward who believe, according to the working of His mighty power (Ephesians 1:17-19).*

Now you must pray for His "wisdom. Believe it, receive it, and know that He is able to do just what He said He would do. So go **lean** down with the guidance of the Holy Spirit, and begin picking up some lost pennies today, amen……

Lifting

Now "*lifting*" up these lost and worthless "pennies" from the ground became a very important step in my understanding also. It "teaches" the believer how our God can work, only if we are willing to yield to the power and presence of the Holy Spirit in our lives. What does it mean to *lift* something up? Here is how it is defined in the dictionary: *to raise; to move something from one position to another; or to a higher position.* Wow! The definition speaks volumes in itself, in relation to the responsibility that you and I must assume. Now let us see the correlation with *lifting* things up as it relates to working for the United States Postal Service.

Lifting is just one of the ways, in which we provide quality service for our customers every day. This topic is so important to the Postal Service, that once a year we take a course on proper *lifting* techniques.

.

1. The first thing we learn is to Size up the consignment. Test it to see if you can lift it carefully. Can you grasp it firmly? Get as close to the load as likely before *lifting* it. If possible, slide the load towards you before picking it up.

2. Make sure your footing is secure. Do not *lift* objects that obscure vision and footing.

3. Do not twist while *lifting*!

4. *Lift* smoothly, but not slowly.

5. Organize the work so as to avoid *lifting* from the floor. Use the same principles when lowering or placing the load after *lifting.* Place carefully.

6. Try to avoid carrying the load more than a couple of feet.

That sounds and feels quite complicated? But *lifting* and loading are just some of the job responsibilities of being a mail carrier for the Postal Service. Now how does this tie in with these lost and worthless pennies I have been talking about from the beginning? Well there are several things I would like to *lift* in your understanding at this time. If you can remember a few paragraphs back, I mentioned that *leaning and lifting* were the two most difficult steps to master. My job requires that I do a lot of *leaning and lifting*, therefore my physical state and mental state must always be at its peak. This responsibility of being a mailman is carried out 365 days of the year, saved a few holidays, not counting the seasonal changes that we are challenged with year by year. Also keep this in mind that during the *Christ*mas season we *lift* more boxes than any other time of the year. So *lifting* becomes a word of action. Please continue to *lift* with me as the Holy Spirit *lifts* you and me into the presence of our wonderful Savior. If you and I were to take a good look back over our lives, we would discover that God is, has, and will always be a God of *lifting* up. This enlightening truth about God is revealed when we take a close look at Jesus. Did you know that you and I have been blessed with every spiritual blessing from the Father? I will come back to that with a word from the Lord in a few moments. But here is the first truth that you and I must know and understand for ourselves about our God in conjunction to His word. So I need you to remember that the word *lift* means: to *lift* something from one position to another, or higher. I am attempting to conclude this topic, but the Holy Spirit is holding me hostage at this moment—and for good reasons. For you see, the bible declares a wonderful truth about Jesus.

> *Wherefore God also hath highly exalted Him, and given Him a mane which is above every name: that at the name of Jesus every knee should bow, of things in heaven, and things in earth, and things under the earth; And that every tongue should confess that Jesus Christ is Lord, to the glory of God the Father (Philippians 2:9-11).*

Then as we read *Romans 10:9,* it shares with you and me a life saving and changing truth.

> *That if thou shalt confess with thy mouth the Lord Jesus, and shalt believe in thine heart that God hath raised Him from the dead, thou shalt be saved.*

And because we have this wonderful gift from God, which is in Christ Jesus, we have been blessed with every spiritual blessing from the Father. I mentioned to you a few lines back that I would come back to that question about being blessed with all spiritual blessing. And here is why, because God is revealing through His word at this very moment. All we need to do is believe it and receive. He then can *lift, raise* and position us in the way that He would have us to follow, amen. Let us read His word together as He speaks.

> *Blessed be the God and Father of our Lord Jesus Christ, who hath blessed us with all spiritual blessings in heavenly places in Christ. According as he hath chosen us in Him before the foundation of the world, that we should be holy and without blame before Him in love. Having predestinated us unto the adoption of children by Jesus Christ to Himself, according to the good pleasure of His will, To the praise of the glory of His grace, wherein He hath made us accepted in the beloved. In whom we have redemption through His blood, the forgiveness of sins, according to the riches of His grace; Wherein He hath abounded toward us in all wisdom and prudence; Having made known unto us the mystery of His will, according to His good pleasure which He hath purposed in Himself; That in the dispensation of the fullness of times He might gather together in one all things in Christ, both which are in heaven, and which are on earth; even in Him (Ephesians 1:3-10).*

Now you and I have not received these spiritual blessings for self gain. It is so we may be a blessing to someone else whom we might help to *lift, raise,* and move in the direction of Christ, so that He may take them *higher*. How, then, and why is Christ so able to *lift, raise* and take you and me *higher*? I am so glad you *lifted* that question in your hearing as the Holy Spirit brings this section to its conclusion. However please keep in mind what we are talking about. We are still talking about lost and worthless pennies, which I would *lift* from the ground on my route each and every day. I first shared with you a made up word called *loolealif,* which really means to *look, lean, and lift*. I then gave you a breakdown of each word in relation to my job experience and then according to the word of our God. And now we are ready to conclude with the *lifting* aspect of this section. These words will come right from the lips of our Savior, here we go.

> *And I, if I be lifted up from the earth, will draw all men unto me (John 12:32).*

The Holy Spirit is yet still holding me hostage, so as to make sure that the negotiations of His word is precise and clear to all who may be reading this book. Now let us break this verse down together with the *lifting* power of Jesus. As I would *look, lean, and lift* these lost and worthless pennies from the ground, here is the first revelation God unveils. He speaks in this comportment: *And I, if I be lifted up from the earth,* stop right there. Every day that the Lord blessed me to carry out my job responsibility, here is what I have discovered as we read this text together. The word *I* signifies one. So John repeats this again so as to make sure that there is only one who should be *lifted* up in our talking, walking, and living. Need proof about Him being one? Here it is according to God's eternal word:

> *One Lord, one faith, one baptism, One God and Father of all, who is above all, and through all, and in you all (Ephesians 4:5-6).*

Now as we take a look at the very next words, it reads *if I be lifted up from the earth.* All of these lost and worthless pennies came from the ground—meaning the earth. Normally people do not pick things up from the ground, for we consider the ground to be dirty and unsanitary. So in most cases, if we see a lost and worthless penny on the ground or in the dirt, we will not hesitate to move on. But I mentioned to you from the offset of this section that *lifting* was a difficult step to master—for it would always challenge me to pick up the lost penny. But I soon realized that God was ordering my steps, not me. So learning to *lift* these lost and worthless pennies up became a part of my God given responsibility every day. This was a choice that I needed to make in order to understand this wonderful revelation from our God. How about you? Are you willing to make a choice for the cause of Christ? Only you know the answer to that question, amen?

Now let us continue so that we may bring this section to its final negotiations as the Master concludes with the final words in this verse, *will draw all men unto me.* Did you know that Jesus had a certain charisma about Him that would cause people to follow Him everywhere He went? How about you and me? Do we have the spirit of Christ in our hearts that would cause people to follow us, as we follow Him? Only you know the answer to that question. Well I want to take a moment and converse on this question from the word of God. Did you know also that the Apostle Paul had this same magnetizing effect on people? But this was only possible because of the faith that he had in the risen Savior. The Apostle Paul understood that, in order to compel people he needed to first meet them where they were. Here is what he declares about this wonderful truth in his life, according to his first letter to the church at Corinth.

> *For though I be free from all men, yet have I made myself servant unto all, that I might gain the more. And unto the Jews I became as a Jew, that I might gain the Jews; to them that are under the law, as under the law, that I might gain them that are under the law; To them that are without law, as without law, (being not without law to God, but under the law to Christ,) that I might gain them that are without law. To the weak became I as weak, that I might gain the weak: I am made all things to all men, that I might by all means save some. And this I do for the gospel's sake, that I might be partaker thereof with you (1 Corinthians 9:19-23).*

Now here in this scripture you will discover that the Apostle Paul uses the word *gain* which means to increase, progress, attain more, or reach; in other words he became a servant to all. What a blessing the Apostle Paul has become because of the faith that he had in Jesus. But our loving Savior epitomizes this truth, while foretelling how He would be crucified on an old rugged cross for my sake and yours. We took a look at it already. He declares that:

> *and I, if I be lifted up from the earth, will draw all men unto me (John 12:32).*

Jesus truly is the "neodymium" of today, yesterday, and tomorrow. For you see "neodymium" is one of the most powerful materials used for making strong magnets. And our loving Savior has this very same powerful magnetizing effect on people when they meet Him for the first time. So that is why I am so excited about what God has done through His Son Jesus, because this same magnetizing effect has been made available for you and me through the power and presence of the Holy Spirit. So much so, that I made up my mind to *lift* up every penny I see on the ground without any reserve, amen. Will you join me in this wonderful revelation from our God? Will you move out of the state of complacency and allow God to finish what He has begun in your life? And more importantly, will you trust God for the great things He has done, will do, and for what He is doing right at this moment, as you read this book? I pray that at this second pivotal point of this wonderful revelation some things are becoming clearer to you by our God's unlimited grace Amen.......

The state of urgency explained

I mentioned the *state of urgency* a little earlier in the beginning of this wonderful revelation from our God. Exactly what does that mean? Well, I am glad you asked! Now keep in mind what the scriptural text for this whole revelation reveals. *In Matthew chapter 28:19a,* as we read again, **Go ye therefore,** which says to the believer or believers, yes even the body of Christ—before you go you must be able to see a need to go. Just like so many of these worthless pennies that I found, I saw a great need to rescue them out of their loss state of being. Watch how scripture will once again bring this reality into focus and point out the gravity of their state or condition. In the book *of Jude verses 20 thru 23, we read),*

> *But ye, beloved, building up yourselves on your most holy faith, praying in the Holy Ghost, Keep yourselves in the love of God, looking for the mercy of our Lord Jesus Christ unto eternal life. And of some have compassion, making a difference: And others save with fear, pulling them out of the fire; hating even the garment spotted by the flesh.*

Oh my Jesus of everlasting life! There is power in the word of our God. You and I have the answer right here in *Jude verse 23.* Let us read His word together again, ***and others save with fear, pulling them out of the fire.*** That's why the *state of urgency* is so vital to our understanding. Why, because someone might burn to death. You see firemen are trained to go into burning buildings, in spite of the dangers which lie before them. But they still press on to save any life that may be alive in the fire. Well this is what this verse is saying to you and me. We must look at this worthless penny as a life that needs to be saved from a burning hell that God never intended for his creation in the first place. It was designed for Satan and his hellish imps. Not to get off course, but if you and I will become conscience in our needing to understand this, we will discover that there is somebody down in the valley trying to get home. Only then will we see the importance of going. If we were to be very honest with ourselves, we have a loving Savior who searched until He found our wandering souls (lost pennies). Christ Jesus our lord had a purpose in mind when He came to this earth. *Dr Luke* reports it in this comportment,

> *For the Son of man is come to seek and to save that which was lost (Luke 19:10).*

So our wonderful Savior not only saves the lost soul, but He continually seeks. He becomes the seeker of our souls. And because this is true it motivates me, it pushes me, and compels me to seek out any lost pennies that appear in my eye sight, amen. Now let's talk about some things related to *state of urgency.* These pennies that I found didn't cause the condition they were in, instead it was the result of man's misusage. What do I mean by that statement? Well anytime we receive too much of something, we tend to take it for granted. If you can remember, the penny started out as pure gold, then the

Anglo Saxons realized that gold was too expensive and hard to find, so they used less pure gold. Copper was then introduced. After copper, came bronze which in turn was mixed with a little tin, and zinc. So we see how the penny started out as pure gold, but then ended up as bronze. Why? Because man had discovered that bronze was easy to find, and in turn could produce more pennies. Well if only you and I would adopt this same approach and recognize this truth. We too can discover many lost souls in the world today. But I was determined in my heart, mind, body and soul to be intentional in my searching and seeking. Why? Because I recognize that every day there would be more lost pennies to be found. So I became very focused on the purpose which was finding these lost and worthless pennies which had little value to so many people. Now being a mailman has taught me some very valuable lessons over time. Our mind set is that of, the mail must be delivered no matter what Mother Nature has in store. We are taught to deliver every piece of mail that is in our possession and we do so day in and day out. Now if it has become that important for me in relation to this job of delivering the mail, then how important is it for us to make clear to the lost souls in the world today that it is our God's desire to deliver all from the hands of darkness, so that he or she may be saved. Please hear me as I will make every attempt to bridge every gap of our thinking process concerning these lost and worthless pennies.......

Now as one begins to have a closer walk with the Savior, he or she becomes more in tuned to their surrounding, and environment. You learn to see things through the eyes of the Savior and you learn to assess every situation around you. One day I took notice of an elderly lady walking down some of the same streets that I work on every day. Apparently, she had a daily routine of walking, so as to keep an active and healthy lifestyle. She always had a very slow one-two step, but she managed to get along just fine. This particular day, we just happen to meet up at the very same spot on the side walk near a patch of browning dry grass. There on the grass laid two lost pennies. But as soon as I made my move to rescue them, she picked the pennies up and proceeded to walk as if nothing happened. This troubled me and it really *stirred up my spirit.* But all I could think about at that moment was that the two pennies should have been rescued by *me.* It was almost as if she snatched them right out of my hand. I felt as if I had failed them. Pity and sorrow fell on me for a few moments, but I had to stay focused on the task because there were so many other pennies scattered around that needed to be saved. *Listen to me!* I am talking as if these lost and worthless pennies have meaning, value, and life. Well the reason being is because my thinking process has changed concerning how I perceive these lost and worthless pennies. If I could learn to feel and think this way about a penny, surely a lost soul in the world today should cause me to go the extra mile. But, I could learn a very valuable lesson from this occurrence. *Just as God is always "searching and seeking" for lost souls, the enemy is always walking to and fro also.* Please understand me. I used the elderly lady as an example for you and me, so as to *stir up the gift of God that is in you.* This made me more determined to let the Lord guide me every step of the way. All too many times, we do not exhibit the gift or gifts that God has placed in our being. All He desires is for you and me to be used by Him. I can remember when I was a young boy, and when I turned a certain age I thought I was grown. One day my father asked me to do something and I took my sweet little time. Well, I do not think that it is important to give you the logistics or the details of that occurrence. But one thing I will share is that when he had finished laying his holy hands on me, it really stirred up my spirit. I discovered that I had many hidden gifts, one being that of the gifts of helps (laugh). The Apostle Paul penned this same truth in scripture for young Pastor Timothy, not so much in the manner that I penned it, but this is how it was written to young Pastor Timothy for future references.

> He writes: *wherefore I put thee in remembrance that thou stir up the gift of God, which is in thee by the putting on of my hands. For God hath not given us the spirit of fear; but of power, and of love, and of a sound mind (2 Timothy 1:6-7)*

So now I pray that you may allow God to stir up the gift, or gifts that He has placed in you. And understand that no matter what our **state of urgency** may be, He is able to save us. So go and use your gift or gifts, as you search for lost pennies today, amen.

Compassion, Humbleness, and Joy

I would like to take some time in this next section, to cover three critical principles that must be understood as we move forward in searching for these lost and worthless pennies. One is having *compassion,* two being *humble*, and three having *joy* that is unspeakable. Now let us begin with our supreme exemplar when it comes to having a true understanding of *compassion.*

> *And Jesus went about all the cities and villages, teaching in their synagogues, and preaching the gospel of the kingdom, and healing every sickness and every disease among the people. But when He saw the multitudes, He was moved with (compassion) on them, because they fainted, and were scattered abroad, as sheep having no shepherd. Then saith He unto His disciples, the harvest truly is plenteous, but the laborers are few. Pray ye therefore the Lord of the harvest, that He will send forth laborers into His harvest.*

That was *Matthew 9:35-38.* Please keep in mind what this entire revelation from God entails about these lost and worthless pennies that I found. *They had no owner and no spender.* But thanks be to God for His Son Jesus. For the bible declares that He was moved with **compassion** for the people. You see, Jesus is able to see right through our soil beings and only He knows just what we need and when we need it. How about you and me? Do we have **compassion** for humanity, or do we just concern ourselves with our own lives and our own well being. Now for the sake of understanding, let's take a look at the Greek grammar for the word **compassion**, as used in *Matthew 9:36*. It is **"splagchnizomia"** and can be defined in this way: *to be moved as to one's inwards, or to have the bowels yearn, feeling sympathy or pity.* Now there is always a down pouring flow of life giving waters that constantly surges from the eternal word of our God. I would like to look at another scripture that should move all believers in Christ Jesus out of their comfort zones and comfort homes. Now no one wants to consider him or herself to be a bad person. We all would like to believe that we are good people, and for the better part we are. But sometimes life will challenge us in relation to who we say we are and who we claim to be. Jesus tells this parable of the *Good Samaritan* in *Luke 10: 30-37:* He shares three examples to examine, so that we may be able to discern their differences in this parable. It starts out in this way*:*

> *And Jesus answering said, A certain man went down from Jerusalem to Jericho, and fell among thieves, which stripped him of his raiment and wounded him, and departed, leaving him half dead. And by chance there came down a certain priest that way: and when he saw him, he passed by on the other side. And likewise a Levite, when he was at the place, came and looked on him, and passed by*

43

on the other side. But a certain Samaritan, as he journeyed, came where he was: and when he saw him, he had compassion on him. And went to him, and bound up his wounds, pouring in oil and wine, and set him on his own beast, and brought him to an inn, and took care of him. And on the morrow when he departed, he took out two pence, and gave them to the host, and said unto him, Take care of him; and whatsoever thou spendest more, when I come again, I will repay thee. Which now of these three, thinkest thou, was neighbor unto him that fell among the thieves? And he said, He that shewed mercy on him. Then said Jesus unto him, Go, and do thou likewise.

So again I would like to heave this question in your reading at this moment. Do we have **compassion** for others that are lost in the world today? Or do we remain in the same state of being and never truly experience the true movement of the Holy Spirit in our lives? Just as Jesus was moved with **compassion** for the people in *Matthew 9:36,* he epitomizes the importance of having **compassion** for others. He not only feels and sees our condition, but He takes action. I can't even begin to stress the many opportunities that I missed out on, in relation to witnessing for my Lord. Please hear me, it is not mine to have a pity party, but you and I must learn that we are not perfect; we are forgiven. Maybe you found yourself in this same place before like me. You shared the truth of our Lord Jesus with someone. You believed that you were *compassionate* for the concerns they related to you, but you did not take action. Why? Only you know the answer to that question. But whether we respond or not, I pray that each opportunity will hopefully allow us to take a closer look at ourselves and our lives on this journey. So I would like to encourage your heart in realizing that God is still growing, developing, changing, correcting, and more importantly, He still wants to use you and me. I believe that all believers in Christ feel *compassionate* about something. Whether it's our jobs, homes, or our families, the list is limitless. Agreed, we all are *compassionate* about something. But God has a much bigger picture in mind when He speaks of *compassion.* Listen again to the scriptural text, shared in the beginning of this wonderful revelation.

> *Go ye therefore, and teach all nations (Matthew 28:19a).*

Now you tell me, how big is the picture to God, as opposed to what we see? Now there is always harmony in scripture. Listen to the answer Jesus provided for the lawyer, in *Luke 10:37b.* Then Jesus said *Go, and do thou likewise.* This word *Go* is yet another pivotal point of this wonderful revelation from our God. Jesus proclaimed *Go ye therefore,* with *compassion* and love for our Father's business, and He promises that He will be with us *always, even unto the end of the world, amen.* I yet again feel a tugging from the Holy Spirit which is convicting me, even at this moment, because I realize that at times I too fall short in relation to being an effective witness for Christ. But I thank God for His longsuffering, and the "provisional guidance" that He continues to provide for His children, which teaches me not to think of it as a sense of *perfect time,* but as a sense of the *perfect divine.* So when the believer in Christ truly comes to understand this truth. We will then be compelled to move out of the natural state of thinking, such as thinking about oneself and one's own well being.

> *Let every one of us please his neighbor for his good to edification. For even Christ pleased not Himself (Romans 15:2-3a).*

Now for the sake of my own inner argument, please allow me to share this. I do understand that there are some people who we need to be firm and straight to the point with. In the book of *Jude* he makes this very clear as he affirms this truth in *verses 22 and 23.*

> It begins in this manner, *and some have compassion, making a difference: And others save with fear, pulling them out of the fire; hating even the garment spotted by the flesh.*

You know the more I study the word of our God, I am yet convicted, convinced and compelled all at the same time. Here is what I have come to realize in my own imperfections, that I must learn to be obedient to His life changing word. Jude declares that we should save others with fear, pulling them out of the fire, hating even there garments spotted by the flesh. Please follow me again as I follow the pulling power of the Holy Spirit. Some people may not desire to be saved. For we all have our reasons for such thinking. But I believe it is a lack of knowledge, understanding, and the internal and eternal ramifications of sin. As for we who are saved by God's wonderful love thought in this same manner before being saved also. You know it is amazing as I look back over my life. I see how my thinking affected my thought process in relation to the gift by which God provided through His Son Jesus. This gift was free, and we paid nothing for it. But Christ paid it all in full so that we who are lost might be brought back to the Father's eternal love. Jesus did this by shedding His blood on Calvary's cross. All of my sinful acts against the Father would no longer bind me to death eternal. I now have life eternal because of Jesus. But I would have not realized such a wonderful truth if another believer had not witness to me with *compassion* and in love. I once thought that if I was a good person, I would have access to life eternal for sure. But this was far from the truth. I also believed that if I minded my own business, went to work every day, and took good care of my family, I would surely be considered a good person according to "society"—all would be well. This type of thinking must be deleted from the way we perceive our God. Jesus proclaims it this way in the account of *Mark 2:17:*

> *When Jesus heard it, He saith unto them, "They that are whole have no need of the physician, but they*

that are sick: I came not to call the righteous, but sinners to repentance."

And because we all are sinners saved by God's wonderful grace, we must respond by telling someone else (meaning a lost soul in the world today) about the good news of Jesus the Christ. Again for my own inner argument, I can hear the voice of Jesus as He sent the twelve out for service. In *Dr. Luke's account Chapter 9:5,* it speaks, of always moving forward, not backwards:

Jesus speaks, *"and whosoever will not receive you, when ye go out of that city, shake off the very dust from your feet for a testimony against them."*

But this I pray, that your testimony may be real and convictional, all at the same time, so as to win lost souls for His cause. Why?

Because it is our God, *who will have all men to be saved, and to come unto the knowledge of the truth (1 Timothy 2:4).*

Compassion continues . . . . Do you ever wonder why certain things from your past seem to remind you of right now? I say that because no one can set you up for the future like God can. *(Go ye therefore.)* I can remember some years ago a young brother who had given his life over to Christ and was just so excited about what the Lord had delivered him from. He would share the good news everywhere he went, with everyone. I remember it so plainly because I had just began working for the post office that covered my town. I was walking and delivering the mail that day when he stopped me and said "Could I ask you a question?" My whole disposition changed at that moment, I said "Yeah" with an attitude *(lost penny*) but he paid my attitude no mind. He asked me if I was saved. I paused for a moment… and then I said yes with my mouth, but I told not the truth in my heart *(lost penny).* What could have caused me to say yes to a question that I really did not understand? *(Lost penny)* It was really a result of the sin that was in my life that I could not see, hear, or understand. Why where these three not apparent at the time when the young brother asked me that question? The answer is revealed in the gospel of *Matthew 13:10-15* by Jesus through this parable:

> *And the disciples came, and said unto Him, Why speakest thou unto them in parables? He answered and said unto them, Because it is given unto you to know the mysteries of the kingdom of heaven, but to them it is not given. For whosoever hath, to him shall be given, and he shall have more abundance: but whosoever hath not, from him shall be taken away even that he hath. Therefore speak I to them in parables: because they seeing see not; and hearing they hear not, neither do they understand. And in them is fulfilled the prophecy of Esaias, which saith, By hearing ye shall hear, and shall not understand; and seeing ye shall see, and shall not*

perceive: For this people's heart is waxed gross,
and their ears are dull of hearing, and their eyes
they have closed; lest at anytime they should see
with their eyes, and hear with their ears, and should
understand with their heart, and should be
converted, and I should heal them.

This is some powerful stuff. God's word is so mind
blowing, but yet convictional all at the same time. I pray
that you will read this scripture with all of your heart, mind,
body, and soul, amen. Now back to the young brother's
question. Do you remember when I shared with you a few
lines back in relation to our God setting me up for his
future work? Well some years later, after I had accepted
Jesus as my personal Savior, the Lord blessed me to have
another encounter with this brother and his state of being
became a *state of urgency (lost penny).* He had fallen back
into a life of drugs, *(lost penny)* and I felt **compassion** fall
all over me. I said to him that I needed to ask him a
question now. *"Do you remember some years ago when*
you asked me a question in relation to salvation?" He
nodded his head with a slow up and down yes. I told him
that I needed to apologize to him. He asked what for, and I
said. "Do you remember some years ago when you asked
me was I saved?" He said yes I do! I then told him that I
lied to him. Tears ran down his face as he looked at me
with sorrow. I asked him not to cry because his labor was
not in vain, because I could say with grand assurance today
and until…..no let me say it the way the preacher would

proclaim it. Do you believe in the Father? Yes I do. Do you believe that He loved you and me so much that He sent His only begotten Son to die for my sins, your sins and the world? Yes I do. Do you believe in the Trinity, which is the Father, the Son, and the Holy Spirit? Yes I do. How long are you willing to believe? Until I die. Then the preacher would run by *Romans chapter 10:9:*

> *That if thou shalt confess with thy mouth the Lord Jesus, and shalt believe in thine heart that God hath raised Him from the dead, thou shalt be saved.*

Now by your own profession of faith thou art saved by the blood of Jesus, amen. I almost received Jesus as my personal Savior again that day (laugh). Back to the story, the brother stood up wiped his tears, and exclaimed to me that he was going to get the necessary help that was needed to get his life back on track. The Lord used me at that moment, just like he used the brother some years back to witness to me. The only difference was that he was receptive and I was not. But our God is so patient, kind, and loving that He is willing to give you and me another chance to hopefully get it right for the glory of His name.

> For it is our God, *who will have all men to be saved, and to come unto the knowledge of the truth (1 Timothy 2:4).*

This is a major pivotal point of this God given revelation we must see and understand. From the beginning, I talked about these lost and worthless pennies I found all over my route. And now I am talking to you about lost souls in the world today. So please have *compassion* as you talk to others about the goodness of Jesus, amen.

Humility

Now it's time to talk about being **humble,** as it relates to our being effective witnesses for the cause of Christ. This will be another connection that must be understood as we move forward in finding these lost and worthless pennies. Our "Lord and Savior" was **humble** in every way. Christ is our supreme example and He teaches us how to be **humble** just as He was. I would like to focus on this word **humble** for a few moments, so as to bring some clarity concerning this subject. The Webster's dictionary defines the word **humble** as, having or showing a consciousness of one's short comings, or to lower in condition or rank. Now the word **humble** is translated from the Greek word *tapeinoo (pronounced tap-i-no-o) which means to assign a lower rank or place.* Now, we should always be mindful, of the God that we serve in relation to **humbling** ourselves in His presence. I want to share with you some wonderful mind changing scriptures from the word of our God in conjunction with being **humble.** In the book of *Romans, chapter 12:16,* we hear the apostle Paul saying.

> *Be of the same mind toward one another. Do not set your mind on high things, but associate with the* **humble***. Do not be wise in your own opinion.*

This truth was so real for **James** that he mentioned it twice in *chapter 4:6b, and verse 10.* He writes in verse 6b,

God resists the proud, but gives grace to the **humble**.

In verse 10, he writes:

Humble *yourselves in the sight of the Lord, and He will lift you up.*

In first Peter, we find that he too was in tune with the Apostle Paul as well as James. The Apostle Paul declares that we should not set our minds on high things of this world, but be of the same mind. And I do believe Peter realizes this same truth about our God. Listen to what he writes in *1 Peter 5:5-6:*

> *Likewise you younger people, submit yourselves to your elders. Yes, all of you be submissive to one another, and be clothed with* **humility**, *for "God resists the proud, but gives grace to the* **humble.**

In verse number 6, he echoes the same sounds of James with the pitch being the guide:

> *Therefore* **humble** *yourselves under the mighty hand of God, that He may exalt you in due time.*

With this being the truth, why do we not remember to **humble** ourselves before God and man? Once again I can hear the apostle Paul as he amplifies his tone in *Romans Chapter 12:3:*

For I say, through the grace given to me, to everyone who is among you, not to think of himself more highly than he ought to think, but to think soberly, as God has dealt to each one a measure of faith.

Now I shared several scriptures with the intent of awakening your sense of **humbleness.** Please take this into consideration also, that **humbleness** can be a process taught from one's own personal experiences in life. But true **humbleness** can only be taught by knowing the true teachings of Christ. I believe if we were **humble** toward our God and one another, there would be no need for the Apostle Paul to elaborate continually and so perpetually on this topic. Now there is one thing I noticed, in relation to many of these worthless pennies that I found. I first had to learn how to **humble** myself to bend down and pick them up. Why are we so ashamed sometimes to bend down and pick these worthless pennies up? Please stay with me again as I follow the direction of the Holy Spirit. Now, there is always one main reason why most of us will not stop to bend down and pick up this worthless penny that I am speaking about. Are you ready for the answer? Well here it is—someone may be watching. So infamy wins the battle in many instances. And even though we are able to see the penny and pick it off the ground, we will not because of the infamy we feel on the inside. But for me it became a learning process as I continue to walk in **humility** before our God and man, amen………

JOY

There is a song we sing every so often, during our praise and worship moment, and it begins in this comportment: ♪*This joy I have the world didn't give it to me. Ooh this joy I have the world didn't give it to me. This joy I have the world didn't give it to me ooh no! The world didn't give it and the world can't take it away*♪... But what is true *joy* in the life of the believer that is in Christ Jesus? First, let us define this word together, so as to obtain some clarity regarding *joy.* The word "*joy*" comes from the Greek root word *chara:* **and means to be exceedingly glad.** So am I to be exceedingly glad while searching for these lost and worthless pennies on my route every day? And the answer is yes! Did you know that the Master in His high priestly intercessory prayer prayed to the Father that you and I might have *joy* everlasting in Him? Listen, as He speaks through His word:

> *And now come I to thee; and these things I speak in the world, that they might have my **joy** fulfilled in themselves. I have given them thy word (John 17:13-14a).*

Our loving Savior prayed that we might have our *joy* fulfilled in Him, while on this journey called life. There is nothing that can ever compare to what is meant in this high priestly prayer offered by the Savior on our behalf. He knows that we will be knocked down, but we can get back up because of

Him. He knows that sorrow will knock on our doors regularly, but He wipes away the tears. And He also knows that we can find perfect *joy* in knowing Him through His word. Here is the key that unlocks this truth in this scripture. Jesus says something that follows after verse number 13 in this Gospel of John, which helps to sum up the *joy* that is in Him:

I have given them thy word (John 17:14a).

Knowing His word is going to make all of the difference on the journey in relation to our keeping His *joy*. And true *joy* can and only will come from knowing Him through His word. Think about this truth for a moment with me. The very first time I found a penny, I was not that excited. I did not have much *joy* because pennies can normally be found anywhere. And we learn very early in life to ignore them when we see them. But once I believed and received this wonderful revelation from our God, it changed my whole perspective about the penny. For I realized at that moment I too was a lost penny, and I wanted to celebrate the *joy* that I had by finding as many lost pennies as I could. You see my *joy,* became an ***out-ward expression, from an in-ward explosion.*** I was so thankful to God for what He so graciously provided through His Son Jesus. This made me more determined to exclaim my *joy* with everyone, anyone and anywhere. So here are the benefits of knowing His word concerning our *joy* in Him. *Psalms 16:11* states,

*Thou wilt shew me the path of life in thy presence is fullness of **joy**; at thy right hand there are pleasures for evermore.*

*Psalms 30:5b states, weeping may endure for a night, but **joy** cometh in the morning.*

*Jeremiah 15:16a states, Thy words were found, and I did eat them; and thy word was unto me the **joy** and rejoicing of mine heart.*

*Romans 15:13 states, Now the God of hope fill you with all **joy** and peace in believing, that ye may abound in hope, through the power of the Holy Ghost.*

But Jesus is our final and supreme example when it comes to truly understanding joy. Here is how the writer to the Hebrews penned it to scripture:

*Looking unto Jesus the author and finisher of our faith; who for the **joy** that was set before Him endured the cross, despising the shame, and is set down at the right hand of the throne of God (Hebrews 12:2).*

And because all of this is true, I will *make a **joyful** noise unto the lord (Psalms 100:1a).* Amen.

Now what do these scriptures have to do with finding lost pennies? And I can tell you for certain, that if there is no *joy* in your serving Him, then it is all for nothing. But when you and I *"change" our perspective* on how we view the world, we then will be able to see things the way God see's them. Let us look and see a very powerful truth revealing scripture as it relates to the sentence we just read. Now will you agree with me that looking, and seeing both mean the same thing? So therefore they are synonyms. In the book of *Hebrews chapter 12:2a,* we find this truth concerning seeing things the way God see's them. But this is only possible by *Looking unto Jesus the author and finisher of our faith.* You see, finding these lost and worthless pennies on my route everyday was very difficult at first. So therefore, I had to learn to "look and see" through the eyes of Jesus. So once again *Hebrews 12:2a* is appropriate at this moment: *Looking unto Jesus the author and finisher of our faith.* And this very same truth is still available to all who will look unto Him for deliverance and salvation. So as you continue to exclaim your *joy* that comes from knowing Jesus, go search for lost pennies everywhere you go, amen . . . .

Just thanking God. Now I am always astonished at the moving power and the presence of the Holy Spirit in my life. I believe that this wonderful revelation is unfolding right before my eyes and all who will desire to see it with me. In the beginning of this wonderful revelation from God, I optimistically shared with you, that by the time we reach the end of this revelation it would all make sense. I really had no idea that I could share so much insight about a seemingly worthless penny. But the Holy Spirit is yet guiding me and directing me every step of the way, and I am so grateful. The *Psalmist* reports it this way in *verse number 8,* of the *thirty second division.*

> *I will instruct thee and teach thee in the way which thou shalt go; I will guide thee with mine eye. Amen.*

Learning

I would like to cap, at this moment, three other principals that would be very helpful and effective as we serve Jesus. But before we do so, allow me to share with you a truth about my walk with Jesus. Jesus truly has been my instructor and my spiritual eye every day. You see, before I begin my route, I have a brief talk with my heavenly Father. I say, lord bless me to find one penny today. You be my arms, legs and eyes so that I may bring glory to your name. And bless God, when I come to the close of another days work, there is more in my pocket than what I asked God for. You may be asking yourself this question in relation to what I just shared. I ask God to bless me to find one penny, so that I may bring glory to His name. How then is it possible to bring glory to God's name by finding one lost penny? I am so glad you thought that question in your mind. Please keep in mind what was shared with you at the offset of this wonderful revelation from our God. I mentioned to you that the "conventional" or "banal" way of thinking needs to be absent if we are going to be able to see, think, and do things differently in our lives. Now let's take a look at three applicable lessons for a few moments, as we learn together. *The first lesson- learning of (Him); second lesson- living for (Him); and the third lesson- finishing because of (Him).* Also, keep in mind that at times I will approach this from a mailman's perspective. I would first like to talk about *learning* one's route. One year while working for the United States Postal Service, we were in a transitional period of downsizing. This meant that all routes would be adjusted, while others would become obsolete. Once the adjustments were made, every route would then be posted for rebidding. This could result in one losing his or her route to someone with more seniority. If this happened a carrier then would have to bid a new route, and *learn* everything pertaining to that new route. Now *learning* a new route at first can be quite a challenge. Here is why: First you need to *learn* all of the numbers that are on the houses, and also the new streets you will be traveling on every day. Second, you need to *learn* where the mailboxes are on every house or business. And third, you need to *learn* every name on each mailbox. Although this process of *learning* and starting all over again may seem a little challenging at first, we *learn* to adjust and perform our task everyday and get the job done. But the key word here is that we have *learned.* So please follow me, as I follow the *learning* route of the Holy Spirit. King Jesus speaks in this comportment,

> *Take my yoke upon you, and learn of me; for I am meek and lowly in heart: and ye shall find rest unto your souls (Matthew 11:29).*

Jesus gives you and me the "blessed" assurance that if we would take His yoke upon ourselves and *learn* of Him, we will then find rest for our wandering souls. You know *learning* about the Savior and His life can be quite amazing, exciting and stimulating all at the same time. But this is only possible when we *learn* of Him, and as a result we are more apt to share our joy, peace, kindness, and love with someone else. Listen, just like the mailman or mailwoman, who walks, talks, and delivers the mail from house to house every day, you also have a daily route or routine. And during that daily routine, you pass by many lost pennies day after day. So why are we not able to see these lost and worthless pennies, or lost souls? For one, we need to *learn* our routes. But let's be honest. Do we really take the time out to know everyone that we pass by on any given day? Now just for insight in relation to *learning* our routes, the Webster dictionary defines the word route in this manner: *a way, road, course, direction, or path*, just to name a few. So a route can be defined as "a way or path". Watch this once again how scripture will bring this "way or path" into focus. In the book of *John chapter 14:6,* we read these words right from our Savior's lips. *Jesus saith unto him, I am the* **way**, *the truth, and the life; no man cometh unto the Father, but by Me.* Here are some more scriptures to support this truth:

> *Teach me thy* **way,** *O Lord, and lead me in a plain path (Psalm 27:11a).*

> *For the Lord knoweth the* **way** *of the righteous (Psalms 1:6a).*

> *This is the* **way,** *walk ye in it, when ye turn to the right hand, and when ye turn to the left (Isaiah 30:21b).*

Now I shared quite a few scriptures with you for a purpose. I want you to understand that *learning* your route will be very crucial, concerning our task of seeking and saving. So please keep in mind what we are talking about; we are talking about *learning* of Jesus. And as a result of *learning* about Jesus, we then can bring glory to God's wonderful name. Did you know that one of the Greek root words for yoke is **Zugos**? Meaning to "couple" or "coupling". You and I should take great delight in knowing that our wonderful Savior wants to couple with sinners like you and me. Let me see if I can explain it another way. Some years ago, I joined a fitness club to stay healthy and active. I soon discovered that most of the times I would go, I was unmotivated and uninterested in working out by myself. I thought, if only I had a partner to work out with, I would get the motivation I needed to get results. So I did just that, I met a partner **(Jesus)** who was willing to help me work-out hard and get the results I needed. My partner **(Jesus)** always made the workout interesting and challenging. He **(Jesus)** knew all of my weak points and yet all of my strengths. And although there were times when I would try to go beyond my limitations, but my partner **(Jesus)** was always there to help me through. So exactly what am I saying? Well Jesus in this *29th* verse of *Matthew chapter 11,* declares that if we partner up with Him, that if we couple up with Him, that if we *learn* of Him, we are guaranteed to see results in our physical lives, and more importantly, our spiritual lives. Did you know that in the fitness world there are several ways in which one can build muscle? The two I know off hand are getting plenty of proteins and plenty of rest. You see proteins help to build muscle, and sleep helps to enhance muscle development. Jesus is all of the proteins which we will ever need to develop our spiritual bodies. And we can find perfect rest in Him, so that our spiritual lives may be enhanced by resting and *learning* of Him. Listen again as He speaks through His Word:

> *Come unto me, all ye that labour and are heavy laden and I will give you rest. Take my yoke upon you, and learn of me. For I am meek and lowly in heart: and ye shall find rest unto your souls (Matthew 11:28-29).*

Will you join me by doing you're very best to learn of Him? If you will, I can tell you with great expectancy that He will do just what He said He would do. And as a result thereof, you will become very effective in "seeking and finding" these lost and worthless pennies. In other words you will be leading lost souls to Christ, because you have *learned* from Him, and of Him. And that is just one of the ways by which we can bring glory to God's wonderful name, amen......

Living

Have you ever heard someone make this statement before: I just want to *live* my life? Well in this next lesson I would like to talk about *living* one's life. I can remember the first time I went out for my training to become a mailman. It was definitely a learning experience for me each day of the process. But in order to secure my job, I needed to complete a 90 day probationary period. This would become a true test of my endurance, stamina and work ethics in learning how to finish the job correctly every day. So when my probationary period came to an end, all I could see and think about was me delivering the mail on my own. I remember looking at my uniform all night long, just to make sure that it was real. I even put the uniform on and pretended like I was delivering the mail. It felt like my first day of grade school. I was just so excited because now I would be *living* the life of a real mailman. *Me*! But the very next day, my true test would come. There were so many factors that I did not consider. First, I was now on my own and had no one to give me guidance or direction. So at times, I would find myself looking for streets, mailboxes, and numbers on the houses, which were not always legible and visible. I discovered that *living* my life as a mailman was going to be a bit more challenging than what I envisioned. I had the uniform, the shoes, the hat and the bag, but something was missing in my new life as a mailman. What could it be? I would soon discover that the life of *living* as a mailman would challenge me to gain more experience in this field of work. I thought I was ready to make my own choices and decisions, but instead I made more mistakes and wrong turns my first couple of weeks of *living* as a mailman.

But really what does it mean to live one's life? This is just another way of declaring some times that we want to be able to make our own choices and decisions in life without the help and guidance of others. Please pay attention, for I will make every attempt to reflect on our fading life choices, and then reflect on the absolute choices of our loving Master. From the time we realize that we are grown, per say, we begin to make decisions for ourselves, and so we *learn* the three any rule plan. *I can go anywhere, I can do anything, and I can be anyone I want to be,* irrespective to the nouns of *life,* meaning any person; any place, or anything. But we, who are saved by God's wonderful grace, have put this nature of thinking behind us. For we have been taught by the loving Master to *live* a life that is entangled in His *life*. So our *living* is to be a life that is *lived* in Him and through Him. Please keep in mind the question I raised in your reading a few paragraphs back. *How do we bring glory to God's name by finding one lost worthless penny?* Well our loving Savior understood this question in relation to His life being glorified through his Father. He was obedient in every way when it came to the Father's will. And as one endeavors to study the word of God, you will discover that Jesus' actions were altruistic. His aim was to always bring glory to His Father's name.

How about you and me, do we live a *life* that is pleasing to the Father, one that brings glory to His name? Jesus provides the answer to this central question in the book of *Matthew 5 verse 16*. We read:

> *Let your light so shine before men, that they may see your good works, and glorify your Father which is in heaven.*

Listen to this short story concerning what was just read. I can remember some years ago, when I was blessed to see a Brian McKnight show live. He gave the performance of his life that night. But now as I reflect back and think about his show, there was one thing I remember in particular. Every time Brian would move on the stage, there would be a large bright light encompassed around him. No matter how fast or how slow he moved, the light would over shadow him. Not only did Brian McKnight give a great performance that night, but the lighting engineers performed a great show as well. Watch this **(thank you Holy Spirit).** Yes Brian McKnight performed that night, flawless and uninterrupted. But if there were no lighting engineers, his performance would have been in total darkness, and no one would have been able to see his performance, talents, yes even his good works that night. So thanks be to the staff and all who played a major role in the stage lighting process that night. Brian McKnight was able to perform another successful show for all to enjoy. So what exactly am I suggesting? Well if you and I want our good works to be visible before men, if we would like to see our lights shining bright in darkness so that God may get all the glory, then we need to understand that Christ is the true lighting engineer. His light should over shadow our lives no matter where we go or what we do. Where does it say that in the scriptures? I am so glad you asked. In the gospel of *John* we can find this truth in *chapter 12:46* as Jesus speaks:

> *I am come a light into the world, that whosoever believeth on me should not abide in darkness.*

In the book of *Ephesians 5:8 and 14*, we can find this truth also:

> *For ye were sometimes darkness, but now are ye light in the Lord: walk as children of light: Wherefore He saith, Awake thou that sleepest, and arise from the dead, and Christ shall give thee light.*

In the new living translation it reads in this comportment, in verse number *14*:

> *Wake up, sleeper, rise from the dead, and Christ will shine on you.*

But Christ is our supreme example, in relation to *living* a life that always glorified the Father's name. In the book of *John 17:1, and 4a*, we read:

> *These words spake Jesus, and lifted up His eyes to heaven, and said, Father, the hour is come; glorify thy Son, that thy Son also may glorify thee; (4a) I have glorified thee on the earth...*

So now this is another way by which we can bring glory to God's name, by finding one lost penny, when we live our lives through and by Christ Jesus, amen.

Finishing

Now in this last lesson we will look at, finishing *the course* so that we may bring glory to God's name. At the United States Postal facility, we have a time clock by which we regulate our clock rings every day. We have a begin tour, a moved tour, and an end tour. Now the beginning tour is important. But the end tour is probably the most important one to supervision. We have eight hours to complete our task. Overtime in most cases will not be authorized without proper instructions from the supervisor. So then what happens to the mail carrier when he or she does not *finish* in a timely manner? They are either reprimanded, whether it is a verbal discussion, or a written resolve. And in some cases they can lose their job if it continues to happen on a regular basis. So it is not so much the begin tour that draws attention, but the end tour. For instance, say if the mail carrier was to bring back first class mail from the street, because he or she could not deliver in the time that was allotted for that day. He or she would then have to fill out the proper documentations, and give reasons why the mail was not delivered for that day. This is frowned upon by management and supervision, as if you are indolent and unwilling to *finish* your job for that day. But thanks be to the God that we serve, for He is a God of completeness. Listen, some days I may not *finish* my route on time, but our God is able to help you and me to *finish* what He has started in our lives. The Apostle Paul writes in this

71

comportment in his letter to the believers in *Philippians 1:6,* we read:

> *Being confident of this very thing, that He which hath begun a good work in you will perform it until the day of Jesus Christ.*

In the New Living translation it reads just a little bit different.

> *Being confident of this, that He who has began a good work in you will carry it on to completion until the day of Christ Jesus.*

Oh, my brothers and my sisters! You need to see, hear, and understand what this scripture is suggesting to the child of God. God can take something out of nothing and create anything He desires. Please hear me at this moment. As I pray that you may be encouraged by this wonderful, but yet inspiring word from our loving Father.

Listen, our *finishing* is really going to be based on three things: our total obedience to the Father's word, will, and way. Please understand these three, as for they will always sing in concert with each other and will always have perfect pitch and harmony in relation to the Father's divine calling on your life and mine. Our God's desire is to *finish* what He has started in our lives. Listen, when the United States Postal Service hired me, they hired me with the understanding that I would be *learning, living, and finishing* their route by their rules and their way. Which is understandable, for it is owned by the highest branch of government in this country, the United States. But we serve a God that is so high, you cannot go over Him; so low, that you cannot go under Him; and so wide, that you cannot go around Him. Here is the truth of this subject matter for you and me. Christ has already *finished* the task for you and me. Please allow me to repeat that phrase. Christ has already *finished* the task for you and me. All we need to do is follow Him and He promises to be with us always.

Do you remember the command we read very early on concerning this wonderful revelation from our God. It was in the gospel of *Matthew 28:20b*. ***I am with you alway, even unto the end of the world.*** Amen. Jesus is the word for all, He is the will of God for all, and He is the way by which all should follow and *finish.* I am so encouraged at this moment that I can hear the Apostle Paul, as though he was right in front of me. He proclaims with great assurance, in Jesus, to young Pastor Timothy this inspiring truth:

> *I have fought a good fight, I have **finished** my course, I have kept the faith (2 Timothy 4:7).*

Notice here that the Apostle Paul *finishes* this scripture with the last word being that of faith–*faith in Jesus*. In the book of *Hebrews chapter 12:2* we find a similar truth concerning faith and *finishing,* it reads in this comportment:

> *Looking unto Jesus the author and **finisher** of our faith; who for the joy that was set before Him*

> *endured the cross, despising the shame, and is set*
> *down at the right hand of the throne of God.*

The writer to the Hebrews also ends with the last word being that of faith. He declares that Jesus is the "Author and Finisher" of our faith. So with that being the truth, "Jesus is, has always been, and will always be the supreme example for all to emulate as a pattern to follow in their life. Let us return to the gospel of *John 17:4 & 19:30b,* so that we may bring this lesson full circle. Now the gospel is the good news, concerning our Lord and Savior Jesus the Christ. I always try to keep this in mind when I study the gospels. Let us read together from the word of our God.

> *I have glorified thee on the earth: I have **finished***
> *the work which thou gavest me to do (John 17:4).*

Now our loving Savior is on the cross of Calvary for my sins, yours sins, and the world's sins. And these were the last three words He spoke while here on this planet called earth—***It is finished** (John 19:30b)*. Now that Jesus has ***finished*** His task before the Father, we can rest assured that God is able to perform in our lives. A ***finished*** look from the corundum's of Christ. So now I pray that you may gain something from the question that was raised earlier. *How do we bring glory to God's name by finding one lost penny?* I have discovered that, learning of Him, living for Him, and finishing because of Him will make this task of finding lost pennies a lot easier every day. I ***finish*** by saying this, ***trust in the Lord with all thine heart; and lean*** *not unto thine own understanding. In all thy ways acknowledge Him, and He shall direct thy paths* *(Proverbs 3:5-6).* Amen.

The Survey

I took it upon myself to do a small survey, concerning these lost and worthless pennies, and I discovered something very unique in itself. When I would ask questions about lost pennies, most people went on the defense; as if to ask me why am I asking such questions. But the Holy Spirit had something totally different in motion. He was showing me another way to approach people with this wonderful revelation from God, so as to get their attention. Now while asking this question in relation to these lost and worthless pennies, I found out that this question peaked some peoples interest and curiosity. Once I planted the seed of thought, I would then leave them to think about what I had shared with them. The question began in this comportment: *When you see a penny on the ground, do you pick it up, all the time, some times, or never?* Then there would be a moment of silence and stillness. I then knew I had their attention. All I was really looking for was an "honest" answer. Now the purpose of a survey is so that one might gain some insight into the subject matter in which he or she is studying. Also, hopefully learn, grow and share, from the information that was collected and taken from the survey. In other words, be a blessing to someone else as you pass along life's way. Go and ask this same question of people, and watch God work. Amen.............

The Penny Revealed....

I pray that at this pivotal point you have come to realize and understand that these worthless and lost pennies I've been talking about really are the lost souls in the world today. After discovering this wonderful truth, my whole thinking process has totally changed. So much so, I find myself looking for pennies all the time—on my job, on my route, at the super market, at the bank, at baseball games—generally everywhere I go. There is one more thing I notice about these lost and worthless pennies. If we take a good look at our coinage system, we will discover that all of the coins are similar in shape. But all of the coins serve one purpose, and that is to pay for something. For you see the world that you and I live in, everything comes with a price tag on it. But thanks be to God for Jesus yet again, for the bible reports:

> *For ye are bought with a price (1 Corinthians 6:20a).*

And because we have been brought with a very high price, we are beholden to Jesus. *So now I am on the battlefield, for my Lord.* You see, you and I have been given a free gift from God. Christ paid the price, but we received the free gift. We created the debt, Jesus made us debt free. And because it was freely given to us, we must freely give it back. Here is how *Matthew* penned it to scripture as Jesus speaks:

77

*Heal the sick; cleanse the lepers, raise the dead, cast out devils: **freely ye have received, freely** give (Matthew 10:8).* Now go, amen.

Recapitulate....... Please continue to follow me as I follow the guidance of the Holy Spirit. I mentioned to you earlier in the book that **looking, leaning, and lifting** would take some time to master in relation to finding these lost and worthless pennies. Once you understand this concept, you will then be more equipped to see the similarities in each coin, which is their round shape. This will not be the case in relation to searching for lost souls; for we are not round, but we all have other similarities. For one, we are all sinners and we all need to be saved from sin.

So the bible declares that, *for all have sinned and come short of the glory of God (Romans 3:23)...*

If we say that we have not sinned, we make Him a liar, and His word is not in us (1John 1:10)....

But thanks be to God yet again, for the bible reports that:

For God so loved the world, that He gave His only begotten Son, that whosoever believeth in Him should not perish, but have everlasting life (John 3:16).

And because all of this is true, I understand my purpose for being saved more so now than I did in the past. How about you? Do you know and understand your purpose for being

saved? *Please allow me to plug this statement at this time. In no way am I suggesting that by finding lost pennies, it becomes our substitute for real battlefield combat.* He has given you and me a charge to keep and a God to glorify, declares the hymn writer. This is about learning how to change our perception and thinking in relation to lost souls in the world today. We always use the word of our God to lead, direct, and guide us in the way that He would have us to follow.

> Again, I quote Jesus as He declares that *I am the way, the truth, and the life: no man cometh unto the Father, but by me (John 14:6).*

So here are the instructions He has left behind for you, me, and the world:

> For the Son of man is come to seek and to save that which was lost (Luke 19:10).

So as believers our main duty is to seek and to save that which was lost. Amen......................................

Details, Details, and more Details...

When one takes a very close look at the penny you will
discover something very interesting in itself. At the top of
the penny, you will see encompassed around it, four small
words engraved, **IN GOD WE TRUST.** Please continue
to follow me, as I follow the guidance of the Holy Spirit.
You see we all have certain things in life that we tend to
pay very close attention to, for whatever the reasons may
be. We look, listen, smell, and taste for diminutive details
concerning the subject matter at that time. And the same is
true of the God that we serve and worship. I will try to
make this clear by sharing some aspects of this word
"detail" as it relates to the God that we love. Now, one can
define the word *detail* in this comportment: *facts, just the
important information, particulars, or fine points,* just to
name a few. So with that being said we must learn to relay
the "facts" or "details" of the information that the Holy
Spirit provides. The bible declares that there are two things
that will happen as a result of our relaying the details of His
story correctly or incorrectly. It will either draw a lost soul
to Christ, or turn them away. Now please allow me to
digress for just a few moments concerning this truth, so that
we may fully understand what I mean when I say that one
or two things can happen.

In the gospel of John you will discover this truth.

*I am come that they might have **life**, and that they might have it more **abundantly** (John 10:10b).*

So Jesus declares that He has come to bring life, and not just a boring stale Christian life, but a life that is to be lived to the fullest, more abundantly in Him. So Jesus is "speaking and teaching" words of life for the saved believer and the unbeliever. Now let us return to my initial statement a few lines back concerning this truth. I mentioned that there are two things that will happen as a result of our sharing the good news or the wrong news. It will either draw a lost soul or lose a lost soul. Please my brothers and sisters think about this statement for just a few moments. You see the second statement suggests that we will lose a lost soul. How deep is that? If we do not share our story with conviction and clarity about what Jesus has delivered us from, the one who is lost could become eternally lost. Wow, what an awesome responsibility the Savior has left us. But not to worry, Jesus has it all figured out through and by His life changing word. So let's use it at this time. Let's go to the book of *Proverbs 18:21.* We read these words:

*Death and life are in **the power of the tongue**: and they that love it shall eat the fruit thereof.*

You and I have the power to speak life or death into our lives and others just as Jesus did. I pray that you may speak life. Now go and share the good news about what Jesus has done for you. Amen..........

Detail 1: Taking a much closer look...

I can remember some time ago when I brought my first car.
It was a 1986 white Volkswagen Scirocco with all black
leather interior. Most of the time, I would find myself
"cleaning and washing" the car to keep it from looking
sullied. You see, white tends to pick up dirt a little easier
than most other colors, and the dirt is more visible to the
naked eye. One day while I was washing the car, I noticed
that there were scuff marks, scratches, and darks spots deep
in the paint that would not come out with a regular sponge
or rag. And that no matter how hard I pressed down on the
sponge or the rag, the spots just would not come out. But I
only noticed the scratches, scuff marks and dark spots when
I was close to the car. But when I would stand just a few
feet back, the scuff marks, scratches, and dark spots seem
to have magically disappeared. In other words it looked
good when I would stand back, but when I would come in
closer it would be more visible. So I called one of my best
friends, who knew a lot about taking care of cars. He said
that I needed to go and have the car *detailed.* I answered
and said, "What's that?" He then went on to explain. He
said that over time weather conditions tend to take its toll
on the cars outside exterior, such as rain, heat, cold
temperatures and other natural elements, which causes
sediments to settle in the paint temporarily and sometimes
permanently, unless some action is taken. He then shared
that the car detailer used a special compound to remove all

of the scuff marks, scratches, and dark spots by going deeper than a sponge or rag could ever go. You see, in this special compound, there is a combination of chemicals that work together to get the job done without damaging the paint on the car. Oh my brothers and my sisters, please continue to follow me as I follow the Holy Spirit. You see God in His perfect love for *detail* did the same for you and me. He used Jesus as His special compound to take out the scuff marks, scratches, and dark spots in our lives so that we may be restored back to our original state of beauty. How does God restore us? I am so glad you asked. You see He can do this in several ways. The first thing God needs to do is to restore us spiritually. The bible declares *God is a Spirit (John 4:24a)*. And because this is true, there can be no restoration of life unless we are spiritually restored. Do you remember the Genesis account in chapter 3 in its entirety? It speaks of sin beguiling the woman in the Garden of Eden to eat from the tree that God forbade. She then in turn gave to her husband, who ate, and death became certain. Well this is what has disconnected you and me from God spiritually. But thanks be to God for His wonderful gift of detail. The bible declares that God loved you and me so much that He gave His only begotten son; He in turn gave His life a ransom for all. You see, when God used His special compound, (Jesus), it had a double effect; it gave us *a new heart and a new spirit (Ezekiel 18:31b)*. Please let us not forget what our objectives are as we read this section, it is to have a closer look at our lives in detail. And yes, we are still talking about lost pennies and lost souls in the world today, amen. But this can and will only happen if we would but allow ourselves to go deeper than what we see in the world today, by learning to pay close attention to detail. Do you remember when I shared with you this statement? That when I would look at the scuff marks, scratches, and dark spots from afar I was not able to see them? But the closer that I moved in, the more visible they became. I then shared with you that the sponge or rag had little if no effect on removing the scuff marks, scratches, and dark spots. Well I am so glad that God is able to see beyond the surface of our lives. Listen as He speaks of this wonderful truth:

> But God hath revealed them unto us by His Spirit: for the spirit it searcheth all things, yea, the deep things of God (1 Corinthians 2:10).

Now please keep in mind what was shared about being restored spiritually. If God is going to reveal himself to you and me, by and through His word, then we need to understand that this can and will only happen by being restored spiritually. And God makes this possible for you and me by believing in Jesus, amen. I want to close this section by sharing the same scripture from the new living translation, but with a different texture. It reads in this comportment:

> For God has revealed them to us by His spirit. The spirit searches all things, even the **deep things of God.** For who knows a person's thoughts except

that person's own spirit within? In the same way no one knows the thoughts of God except the spirit of God. We have not received the spirit of the world but the spirit who is from God, that we may understand what God has freely given us (1 Corinthians 2:10-12).

What a powerful scripture for you and me to absorb, as we continue on this journey with King Jesus, amen...

In God we trust..... As one seriously takes a closer look at the penny, you will discover a very important detail at the top of the penny. It reads IN GOD WE TRUST. I mentioned this subject a little earlier, but I would just like to talk a bit more about this detail. Did you know that the words IN GOD WE TRUST had to be approved by congress to determine if the motto would be appropriate for usage on the American coins? Here are some of other mottos they came up with. {OUR COUNTRY}, {OUR GOD,} and {GOD OUR TRUST}. Now they had the last two correct, but the first one wrong. For you see God is OUR GOD, He is OUR TRUST, and He also is OUR EVERYTHING. I only wished I could have helped in choosing the proper motto. I would have quoted *Matthew in his first chapter verse 23.*

> *Behold, a virgin shall be with child, and shall bring forth a son, and they shall call His name Emmanuel, which being interpreted is, **God with us.***

God has always been with us, and He promises to never leave us or forsake us. What a loving and caring Father we have. And because this is true, we can trust the proverbial writer as he proclaims that we should *Trust in the Lord with all thine heart; and lean not unto thine own understanding (Proverbs 3:5).* So as you and I enter into a war zone of sin and shame, we must never forget that God is with us; every step of the way, amen.

*Who shall separate us from the love of Christ.....*Now please pay close attention, as I attempt to bridge the two together, meaning these lost and worthless pennies and the lost souls in the world today. If you can remember, in the beginning of this wonderful revelation I shared with you some historical facts concerning pennies. The first fact talked about how the penny started out as pure Gold. But as time began to move forward, there would be imitators who soon realized that gold was very expensive and hard to find, so they somewhat watered the gold penny down from its original state. It was transformed from pure gold to bronze which is now worthless to some extent. It fell from the top of the line to the bottom of the line; although it comes from a very rich family of coins. Well in the account of *Genesis chapter 3,* the book of the beginnings, we read a similar story of man's downfall from perfect concord with the Father. His life would become one of "frailty and brokenness" because of peccadillo. That's just a fancy word for sin. But the bible declares that God sent His only Son to be the propitiation for our sins. God loves you, me, and the world so much that He is not going to allow anything or anyone to separate us from His perfect love, no matter how lost we become. The Apostle Paul writes it this way, while raising a very pertinent question for you and me.

> *Who shall separate us from the love of Christ? Shall*
> *tribulation, or distress, or persecution, or famine,*
> *or nakedness, or peril, or sword? For I am*

persuaded, that neither death, nor life, nor angels,
nor principalities, nor powers, nor things present,
nor things to come. Nor height, nor depth, nor any
other creature, shall be able to separate us from the
love of God, which is in Christ Jesus our Lord
(Romans 8:35, 38 and 39).

I pray that we all may enclose our minds and understanding, around such a wonderful truth. Nothing can separate us from the love of God, which is in Christ Jesus our Lord, amen. Take notice of something here with me, if you will, in this account that Paul so compellingly shares. He declares in *verse 35 of this 8th chapter,* **who shall separate us from the love of Christ?** This question will become very important to our understanding as it relates to being an effective witness for Christ. Here is why, because the witnessing we will share will be for the lost pennies, (meaning the lost souls in the world today). Now the enemy will always look for a host to inhabit. And He will use every deception to separate you and me from the love of God, which is in Christ Jesus. Let me see if I can make it lucid. I love to watch the nature channels. I find it to be very relaxing and stimulating all at the same time. Lions are one of the great "land predators" I like to watch in action. Sometimes the camera man would film the lions while they are hunting for prey. They are very intelligent animals. You see when searching for prey they hunt in harmony. Their objective is to separate the weakest animal from the rest of the family. Once they have accomplished such, they will set up an ambush and lure their prey right into a trap of hungry lions. But that does not have to be the outcome for you and me. The Apostle Paul declares that nothing can separate you and me from the love of God that is in Christ Jesus our Lord. So be on your guard! And Stay with the family of God, where there is safety and security. Now go and find some lost pennies, amen............

The Antidote

Antidote, what is it? *A substance that counteracts the effects of a toxin: Something that will take away or reduce the bad effects of something unpleasant or undesirable......*

Now as you go and search for lost pennies, here are some scriptures with the perfect *antidote* to neutralize the enemy when he comes to invade your life—and he will come! The Number one thing we must understand is that we need remember a few scriptures:

Be strong in the Lord and in the power of His might (Ephesians 6:10b).

I can do all things through Christ which strengthens me (Philippians 4:13).

Nay, in all these things we are more than conquerors through him that loved us (Romans 8:37).

Ye are of God, little children, and have overcome them: because greater is He that is in you, than he that is in the world (1 John 4:4).

I pray that at this point you may be feeling the power and the presence of His Holy Spirit working in and through your being. And that as you go and proclaim the word of God, there is a conviction on your heart to win others for the cause of Christ. Jesus understood this very truth about the Holy Spirit working in and through His life. Here is what He proclaims.

> *The Spirit of the Lord is upon Me, because He hath anointed Me to preach the gospel to the poor; he hath sent Me to heal the brokenhearted, to preach deliverance to the captives, and recovering of sight to the blind, to set at liberty them that are bruised, To preach the acceptable year of the Lord (Luke 4:18 and 19).*

His word "speaks and answers" for itself. So now I pray that something was shared in this book that may bless you to hopefully see pennies in a whole new luminosity, as it relates to the many lost souls in the world today.

> Now Lord, ***let the words of my mouth, and the meditation of my heart, be acceptable in thy sight, O Lord my strength, and my redeemer*** *(Psalms 19:14).* Amen...........

The Pot of Gold.... Now you may be wondering to yourself, what happened to all of the lost coins I found, and how much did they total? I will share this with you, whatever the amount may be, all of it will go to the uplifting of God's beautiful Kingdom so that He may receive all the "glory, honor, and praise"—Amen....

I started with the two smaller containers and shortly needed a larger container, which is overflowing as I am writing.